# Baking for Kids

**imagine** THAT!™

This edition published in 2010 for Index Books Ltd.
Imagine That! is an imprint of Top That! Publishing plc.
Tide Mill Way, Woodbridge, Suffolk, IP12 IAP, UK
www.topthatpublishing.com
Copyright © 2010 Top That! Publishing plc
Imagine That! is a trademark of Top That! Publishing plc.

# Contents

## Scrummy Savoury Recipes

## Your Recipes

# Cooking Equipment

*Before you begin to get creative in the kitchen, it's a good idea to take a look through the drawers and cupboards to make sure you know where all the cooking equipment is kept.*

• To complete the recipes in this book, you will need to use a selection of everyday cooking equipment and utensils, such as mixing bowls, saucepans, a sieve, knives, spoons and forks and a chopping board.

• Of course, you'll need to weigh and measure the ingredients, so you'll need a measuring jug and some kitchen scales too.

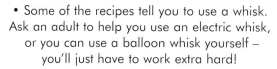

• Some of the recipes tell you to use a whisk. Ask an adult to help you use an electric whisk, or you can use a balloon whisk yourself – you'll just have to work extra hard!

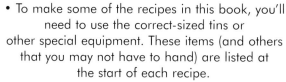

• To make some of the recipes in this book, you'll need to use the correct-sized tins or other special equipment. These items (and others that you may not have to hand) are listed at the start of each recipe.

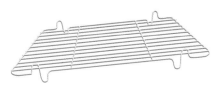

# Safety and Hygiene

*It is important to take care in the kitchen as there are lots of potential hazards and hygiene risks.*

**Take Note!**
Whenever you see the warning triangle you will need adult supervision.

- Before starting any cooking always wash your hands.

- Cover any cuts with a plaster.

- Wear an apron to protect your clothes.

- Always make sure that all the equipment you use is clean.

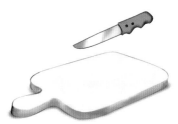

- If you need to use a sharp knife to cut up something hard, ask an adult to help you. Always use a chopping board.

- Remember that trays in the oven and pans on the cooker can get very hot. Always ask an adult to turn on the oven and to get things in and out of the oven for you.

- Always ask an adult for help if you are using anything electrical – like an electric whisk.

- Be careful when heating anything in a pan on top of the cooker. Keep the handle turned to one side to avoid accidentally knocking the pan.

- Keep your pets out of the kitchen while cooking.

# Getting Started

*Baking your own sweet and savoury food is great fun and really quite easy. Best of all, everyone will enjoy what you create!*

## Measuring:

Use scales to weigh exactly how much of each ingredient you need or use a measuring jug to measure liquids.

## Mixing:

Use a spoon, balloon whisk or electric hand whisk to mix the ingredients together.

## Different ideas:

Decorate your cakes and cookies with flavoured or coloured icing, and then add chocolate drops, sweets or sugar strands. Experiment with the savoury recipes to find something you like.

## Different shapes:

Cookie cutters come in lots of different shapes and sizes, and can be bought from most supermarkets. If you don't have any cookie cutters of your own, carefully use a knife to cut out the shapes you want.

## Creating recipes:

Once you've made a recipe in this book a few times, think about whether you could make your own version. Why not mix some chocolate chips into the Coconut Cupcakes mixture or add mushrooms to the Perfect Pizzas? This way you can start to make up your own recipes. Try to think up names for the things you create!

Read through each recipe to make sure you've got all the ingredients that you need before you start.

Always ask an adult for help if you are not sure about anything.

# Yummy Sweet Treats

*Mmm ... bake and taste these mouth-watering sweet treats!*

# Party Buns

*Use lots of brightly coloured icing to decorate these brilliant buns!*

# Party Buns

1. Put the paper bun cases in the bun case baking tray. Sift the flour into a bowl.

**You will need:**
Extra equipment:
paper bun cases
a bun case baking tray
an icing syringe (optional)

Makes
10-12

Ingredients:
225 g (8 oz) self-raising flour
75 g (3 oz) margarine
75 g (3 oz) caster sugar
1 egg
75-100 ml (3-4 fl. oz) milk

Turn to the next page to find out how to make different-flavoured buns.

Preheat the oven to 200°C / 400°F / gas mark 6 ⚠

2. Put the margarine in the bowl. Use the tips of your fingers to rub the margarine and flour together until the mixture becomes crumbly.

3. Add the sugar and mix it in. Now stir in the egg. Finally, add enough milk to make the mixture creamy.

4. Put spoonfuls of the mixture into the paper cases. Bake the buns for 10–15 minutes, until they are golden brown, then leave them to cool on a wire rack.

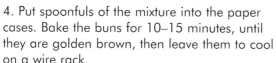
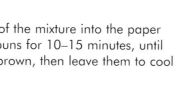

**To decorate:**
for water icing:
100 g (4 oz)
icing sugar
1-2 tablespoons
of water
food colouring

for royal icing:
100 g (4 oz)
icing sugar
1 egg white
food colouring

# Party Buns

## Decorating the Buns

1. Cover the buns with water icing. Here's how to make it! Sift the icing sugar into a bowl. Add 1–2 tablespoons of hot water and mix until you have a smooth thick paste. Add one or two drops of food colouring if you want coloured icing.

To make chocolate icing, add one teaspoon of cocoa powder to the icing sugar before sifting. To make lemon icing, add 1–2 tablespoons of lemon juice instead of hot water.

You can decorate your buns with sugar sprinkles, silver balls or sweets. Once the water icing has set, why not pipe decorations with royal icing?

*Top Tip!*
*Decorate your buns with sugared diamonds, sugar sprinkles, silver balls or small sweets!*

2. To make royal icing, beat an egg white in a small bowl. Sift the icing sugar into the bowl. Beat the mixture until the icing becomes smooth and thick. Add a drop of food colouring if you wish. Spoon the icing into an icing syringe and carefully pipe your decoration onto the buns. Leave the icing to set.

## Variations

### Chocolate Chip Buns

Sift 25 g (1 oz) cocoa into the bowl with the flour. Mix in a handful of chocolate chips. When the buns are cooked and cooled, cover them with chocolate water icing (see method above).

### Coconut Buns

Add 50 g (2 oz) desiccated coconut to the mixture with the sugar. When the buns are cooked, top them with lemon water icing (see method above) and sprinkle them with more coconut.

### Cherry Buns

Add 100 g (4 oz) chopped glacé cherries to the mixture with the sugar. When the buns are cooked, cover them with lemon water icing (see method above) and top each bun with half a glacé cherry.

# Mint Chocolate Cupcakes

*If you like mint and chocolate, you'll love these!*

# Mint Chocolate Cupcakes

1. Put the paper cases in the bun tin.

You will need:

**Extra equipment:**
a bun tin and paper cases

**Ingredients:**
60 g (2 oz) dark chocolate
150 ml (5 fl. oz) water
2 eggs
150 g (5 oz) brown sugar
¼ teaspoon peppermint essence
90 g (4 oz) butter, softened
125 g (4 oz) self-raising flour
2 tablespoons cocoa powder
30 g (1 oz) ground almonds

**For the topping:**
150 g (5 oz) butter, softened
250 g (9 oz) icing sugar
1 teaspoon vanilla extract
2 teaspoons hot water
2 drops of green food colouring
grated chocolate

**Preheat the oven to 175°C /
350°F / gas mark 4**  ⚠

Makes 12

**Take Note!**
Ask an adult to help you melt the chocolate and use the electric whisk.

2. Place the chocolate and water into a small saucepan. Stir over a low heat until melted and smooth. Set aside to cool.

4. Sift in the flour and cocoa. Add the ground almonds. Stir well to combine. Add the warm chocolate to the mixture and stir until just combined.

5. Use a teaspoon to transfer equal amounts of the mixture to the paper cases. Bake the cupcakes for about 25–30 minutes. Leave them to cool on a wire rack.

6. For the topping, beat together the butter and sugar. Once well mixed, add the vanilla essence, food colouring and water. Beat until smooth and creamy. Swirl over your cupcakes. Finish with a few sprinkles of grated chocolate.

3. Place the eggs, sugar, peppermint essence and butter in a large mixing bowl. Beat with an electric mixer until light and fluffy.

# Baked Rice Pudding

*Creamy and filling, this rice pudding will hit the spot!*

# Baked Rice Pudding

You will need:
Extra equipment:
an oven-proof pie dish

Ingredients:
550 ml (1 pt) milk
50 g (2 oz) pudding rice
25 g (1 oz) butter
a few drops of vanilla essence
50 g (2 oz) sugar
grated nutmeg

Preheat the oven to 150°C / 300°F / gas mark 2

⚠️

Serves 4

1. Ask an adult to boil the milk in a saucepan. Then, place the rice in a sieve, wash it well and then sprinkle it into the milk.

2. Add half of the butter, and the vanilla essence, and stir until the milk starts to boil again.

3. Simmer for 3–4 minutes and transfer into a buttered pie dish. Sprinkle with sugar, dot with the remaining pieces of butter and dust with freshly grated nutmeg.

4. Make sure that the edges of the dish are clean and transfer into a preheated oven. Cook until a rich brown skin forms on the top and the rice is cooked through (about 1–1$\frac{1}{2}$ hrs).

# Victoria Sponge

*Make this fab cake for your whole family to enjoy!*

# Victoria Sponge

1. Line the two cake tins with baking parchment.

2. Ask an adult to mix the butter and sugar together with an electric whisk. Next, add the eggs and continue to whisk.

You will need:
Extra equipment:
2 x 18 cm (7 in.) cake tins
baking parchment
electric whisk
sieve
spatula

Ingredients:
100 g (4 oz) butter
100 g (4 oz) caster sugar
2 eggs
100 g (4 oz) self-raising flour
50 g (2 oz) strawberry jam
50 g (2 oz) whipped cream

Serves 12

Preheat the oven to 180°C / 350°F / gas mark 4

**Take Note!** Ask an adult to help you use the electric whisk.

3. Sift the flour into the mixture with a sieve and fold in using a spoon. The mixture should be light and creamy – if it isn't add a drop of milk.

4. Divide the mixture between the cake tins and gently spread out with a spatula.

5. Ask an adult to place the tins in a preheated oven for 20–25 minutes, or until the cakes are golden brown.

6. Add the jam and cream to the top of one cake, sandwich both cakes together, then serve!

# Lemon Poppy Muffins

*These muffins are really light with a zesty lemon zing!*

# Lemon Poppy Muffins

1. Put the paper cases in the muffin baking tray. Ask an adult to help you grate the lemon, but be careful not to grate any of the white pith. Cut the lemon in half and squeeze the juice into a bowl and set aside.

2. Mix together the flour, baking powder, bicarbonate of soda and poppy seeds, and set aside.

3. In a large mixing bowl, cream the butter and sugar together, beating until fluffy. Beat in the eggs one at a time. Add the lemon zest. Beat in half of the dry ingredients and half the yogurt. Now beat in the remaining dry ingredients followed by the remaining yogurt.

4. Spoon the mixture into the paper cases, and bake the muffins for 25–30 minutes, until they are golden brown.

5. While the muffins are cooking, make the topping by putting the icing sugar into the bowl with the lemon juice. Mix them together well.

6. When the muffins are cooked, put them onto a wire rack. While they are still warm, spoon a little of the topping over each one. Leave them to cool.

**You will need:**
Extra equipment:
paper cases
a muffin baking tray

**Ingredients:**
375 g (13 oz) plain flour
1 tablespoon baking powder
1/2 teaspoon bicarbonate of soda
2 tablespoons poppy seeds
140 g (5 oz) unsalted butter
200 g (7 oz) sugar
2 eggs
1 tablespoon lemon zest
350 ml (12 fl. oz) plain yogurt
For the topping:
120 g (4 oz) icing sugar
2 tablespoons fresh lemon juice
Preheat the oven to 190°C /
375°F / gas mark 5

Makes
12-15

Take Note!
Graters are sharp, so take care to mind your fingers!

# Cranberry Orange Cakes

*Munch these tasty cakes as a snack with a drink!*

# Cranberry Orange Cakes

1. Put the paper cases in the muffin tray.

2. Sift the flour, sugar and baking powder into a bowl. Mix them together.

3. Add in the egg, milk and vegetable oil and mix until all the flour is moistened.

4. Fold in the cranberries, orange peel and nuts.

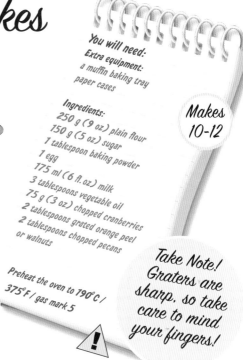

**You will need:**

Extra equipment:
a muffin baking tray
paper cases

Ingredients:
250 g (9 oz) plain flour
150 g (5 oz) sugar
1 tablespoon baking powder
1 egg
175 ml (6 fl. oz) milk
3 tablespoons vegetable oil
75 g (3 oz) chopped cranberries
2 tablespoons grated orange peel
2 tablespoons chopped pecans
or walnuts

Preheat the oven to 190°C /
375°F / gas mark 5

*Makes 10-12*

**Take Note!** Graters are sharp, so take care to mind your fingers!

5. Use a teaspoon to transfer equal amounts of the mixture to the paper cases. Bake the muffins for 20 minutes or until they are well risen and golden brown. Leave them to cool on a wire rack.

# Blueberry Muffins

*These mouth-watering muffins are packed with blueberries!*

# Blueberry Muffins

1. Place the paper cases in the muffin tray.

You will need:
Extra equipment:
a muffin baking tray
paper cases

Ingredients:
50 g (2 oz) butter
2 eggs
200 g (7 oz) sugar
250 g (9 oz) plain flour
2 teaspoons baking powder
100 ml (4 fl. oz) milk
a few drops of vanilla essence
300 g (10 oz) blueberries

Makes
12-15

⚠️

Preheat the oven to 180°C / 350°F /
gas mark 4

2. Add the butter, eggs and sugar to a large bowl. Beat them until well mixed.

3. Mix the flour with the baking powder and sift into the first mixture, alternating with the milk.

4. Blend in the vanilla essence and add the blueberries. Mix everything together until just moistened.

5. Use a teaspoon to divide the mixture equally into the muffin tray. Bake the muffins for 30 minutes or until golden brown.

6. Leave the muffins in the tray until they are cool, and then turn out and enjoy.

# Chocolate Cupcakes

*An irresistible treat for those with a sweet tooth ...*

# Chocolate Cupcakes

1. Put the paper cases in the bun tin.

2. Put the flour, sugar, baking powder, bicarbonate of soda and butter in a large bowl. Mix together.

3. Melt the chocolate in a heatproof bowl over a pan of hot water. Make sure the water doesn't touch the bottom of the bowl.

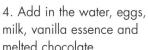

4. Add in the water, eggs, milk, vanilla essence and melted chocolate.

5. With an electric mixer beat at a low speed for 30 seconds. Then beat at a high speed for 3 minutes.

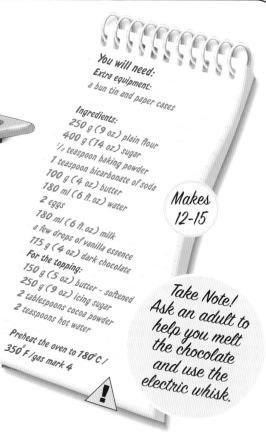

You will need:
Extra equipment:
a bun tin and paper cases

Ingredients:
250 g (9 oz) plain flour
400 g (14 oz) sugar
½ teaspoon baking powder
1 teaspoon bicarbonate of soda
100 g (4 oz) butter
180 ml (6 fl. oz) water
2 eggs
180 ml (6 fl. oz) milk
a few drops of vanilla essence
115 g (4 oz) dark chocolate
For the topping:
150 g (5 oz) butter – softened
250 g (9 oz) icing sugar
2 tablespoons cocoa powder
2 teaspoons hot water

Preheat the oven to 180°C / 350°F /gas mark 4

Makes 12-15

Take Note!
Ask an adult to help you melt the chocolate and use the electric whisk.

6. Use a teaspoon to transfer equal amounts of the mixture to the paper cases. Bake the cupcakes for 20–25 minutes. Leave them to cool on a wire rack.

7. For the topping, beat together the butter and icing sugar. Combine the cocoa powder and water, and add to the mixture. Beat until smooth and creamy. Spread over the cupcakes to finish.

# Orange Cream Cupcakes

If you love orange, you'll love these creamy cakes!

# Orange Cream Cupcakes

1. Put the paper cases in the bun tin.

2. Mix together the flour and baking powder in a bowl.

3. In another bowl, ask an adult to beat the butter and sugar with an electric mixer on a medium speed for 2–3 minutes, until light and fluffy.

**You will need:**

**Extra equipment:**
a bun tin and paper bun cases

**Ingredients:**
190 g (7 oz) plain flour
1/2 teaspoon baking powder
100 g (4 oz) butter
200 g (7 oz) sugar
2 eggs
1 tablespoon orange juice
1/2 tablespoon orange zest
170 ml (6 fl. oz) milk

**For the topping:**
100 g (4 oz) cream cheese
28 g (1 oz) unsalted butter
1 teaspoon orange zest
a few drops of vanilla essence
120 g (4 oz) icing sugar

Preheat the oven to 180°C / 350°F / gas mark 4

**Makes 12-15**

**Take Note!**
Ask an adult to help you use the electric whisk.

4. Add the eggs one at a time, beating well after each one.

5. Beat in the orange extract and zest. On a low speed, beat in the flour and milk, alternating a little at a time. Mix until just combined.

6. Use a teaspoon to transfer equal amounts of the mixture to the paper cases. Bake the cupcakes for 17–19 minutes. Leave them to cool on a wire rack.

7. For the topping, beat together the cream cheese and butter until light and creamy. Add in the orange zest, vanilla essence and icing sugar, beating until smooth. Swirl over your cupcakes and add a sprinkling of orange zest to finish.

# Jammy Roll

*This swirly spiral cake makes a perfect teatime treat!*

# Jammy Roll

1. Put the tin on a sheet of greaseproof paper and draw around it, leaving an edge of 2.5 cm (1 in.). Cut out the paper shape, and make a slit at each corner. Grease the tin with some soft margarine. Now fit the paper into the tin, folding in the edges. Finally, grease the paper with a little soft margarine.

**You will need:**

Extra equipment:
a swiss roll tin 22.5 x 30 cm
(9 x 12 in.)
an electric whisk

Ingredients:
3 large eggs
75 g (3 oz) caster sugar
75 g (3 oz) self-raising flour

For the filling and the top:
3 tablespoons of raspberry or strawberry jam
caster sugar

Preheat the oven to 200°C /
400°F/ gas mark 6

Serves 10-12

Take Note!
Ask an adult to help you use the electric whisk.

2. Break the eggs into a large bowl. Add the sugar, and ask an adult to whisk for a few minutes until the mixture is very light and creamy.

3. Hold the sieve above the bowl and sift the flour into the mixture. Use a tablespoon to stir in the flour, using a gentle figure-of-eight movement – you don't want to knock out the air you've just whisked in!

# Jammy Roll

4. Put the mixture into the tin, and then smooth the top with the back of a tablespoon. Bake for 7–10 minutes, until the edges have shrunk slightly away from the tin. Leave the cake to cool in the tin for 1–2 minutes.

5. Lay out another sheet of greaseproof paper, and sprinkle caster sugar all over it. Whilst the cake is still warm, turn it out onto the paper. Trim off the edges with a knife.

6. Spread the cake with jam. Now roll the cake quite tightly, using the greaseproof paper to help you. Sprinkle some caster sugar over the cake to finish.

*Top Tip!*
*Stand the jar of jam in hot water for about 10 minutes before you need to use it. This will make it easier to spread.*

# Carrot Cake

*This cake is packed with carrots to help you see in the dark!*

# Carrot Cake

1. Put the tin on a sheet of greaseproof paper. Draw around it and cut out the shape. Grease the tin with a little margarine. Put the greaseproof paper inside.

2. Sift the flour and baking powder into a bowl. Add the sugar, nuts, raisins and carrots and stir them together well.

3. Add the eggs and oil to the bowl. Beat all the ingredients together until they are well mixed.

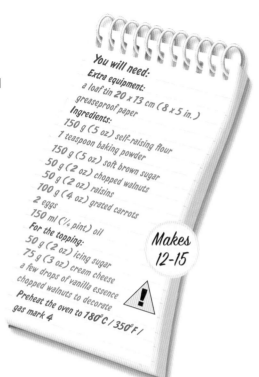

You will need:

Extra equipment:
a loaf tin 20 x 13 cm (8 x 5 in.)
greaseproof paper

Ingredients:
150 g (5 oz) self-raising flour
1 teaspoon baking powder
150 g (5 oz) soft brown sugar
50 g (2 oz) chopped walnuts
50 g (2 oz) raisins
100 g (4 oz) grated carrots
2 eggs
150 ml (¼ pint) oil

For the topping:
50 g (2 oz) icing sugar
75 g (3 oz) cream cheese
a few drops of vanilla essence
chopped walnuts to decorate

Preheat the oven to 180°C / 350°F / gas mark 4

Makes 12-15

4. Spoon the mixture into the prepared tin, spreading it into the corners, and smooth the top with a spoon. Bake the cake for one hour, or until it is firm to the touch.

5. To make the topping, mix the icing sugar, cream cheese and vanilla essence together.

6. Spread the topping mixture over the cake and sprinkle it with chopped walnuts. Keep the cake in the fridge until you are ready to serve it.

# Iced Cookies

*Let your imagination run wild when you decorate these crazy cookies!*

# Iced Cookies

1. Use a paper towel to grease the baking trays with a little butter. Put the butter into a bowl, add the sugar, and mix them together until they're light and fluffy.

**Top Tip!**
Soften the butter by taking it out of the fridge 30 minutes before you need to use it.

**You will need:**
Extra equipment:
2 baking trays
cling film
cookie cutters
rolling pin
an icing syringe

**Ingredients:**
100 g (4 oz) butter
100 g (4 oz) caster sugar
1 egg
225 g (8 oz) plain flour

**To decorate:**
coloured icing (see p. 34)
chocolate chips, sugar sprinkles,
coloured sweets and silver balls

Preheat the oven to 180°C /
350°F / gas mark 4 ⚠

**Makes 10-12**

2. Add the egg, mixing it in well.

3. Sift the flour into the bowl. Gently mix in the flour, and then use your hands to knead the mixture into a smooth dough. Wrap the dough in cling film and put it the fridge for fifteen minutes.

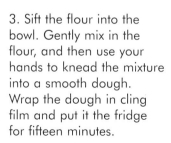

**To decorate:**

| for water icing: | for royal icing: |
| --- | --- |
| 100 g (4 oz) icing sugar | 100 g (4 oz) icing sugar |
| 1-2 tablespoons of hot water | 1 egg white |
| food colouring | food colouring |

# Iced Cookies

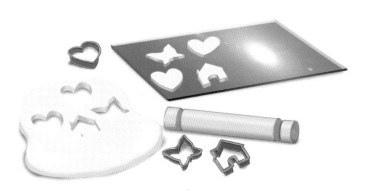

4. Put the dough onto a floured surface, and sprinkle a little flour onto a rolling pin. Roll out the dough (not too thin), and cut out different shapes. Put the biscuits onto a baking tray and bake them for 10 minutes, until they are golden brown. Lift them onto a wire rack to cool.

## Decorating the Cookies:

1. Use water icing to cover the cookies. Sift the icing sugar into a bowl and add enough water to make a smooth paste. Add a drop of food colouring if you want to. To make chocolate icing, add one teaspoon of cocoa powder to the icing sugar. Decorate your cookies with sweets or silver balls, or pipe designs with royal icing.

2. To make royal icing for piping decorations, beat an egg white in a small bowl. Sift the icing sugar into the bowl and beat the mixture until the icing thickens. Add a drop of food colouring if you wish. Spoon the icing into an icing syringe fitted with the nozzle of your choice. Pipe it carefully on to the cookies. Leave it to set.

# Winter Snow Cupcakes

*These cakes will have you walking in a winter wonderland!*

# Winter Snow Cupcakes

1. Put the paper cases in the bun tin.

You will need:
Extra equipment:
a bun tin
paper cases

Ingredients:
150 g (5 oz) butter, softened
150 g (5 oz) sugar
175 g (6 oz) self-raising flour
3 eggs
a few drops of vanilla essence

For the topping:
ready-to-roll fondant icing
blue food colouring

Preheat the oven to 175°C
/ 350°F / gas mark 4

Makes
12

Take Note!
Ask an adult
to help you use
the electric
whisk.

2. Crack the eggs into a bowl and beat lightly with a fork. Add the beaten eggs to a large bowl containing the butter, sugar, flour and vanilla essence.

4. Use a teaspoon to transfer equal amounts of the mixture to the paper cases. Bake the cupcakes for 18–20 minutes. Leave them to cool on a wire rack.

5. Knead a couple of drops of food colouring into half the fondant icing. When the colour is even, roll out the icing and cut out snowflake shapes to cover each cupcake. Decorate with small white icing snowflakes.

3. Beat with an electric mixer for 2 minutes, until the mixture is light and creamy.

# Gingerbread Family

*The delicious gingerbread men are perfect as a bedtime snack!*

# Gingerbread Family

1. Use a paper towel to grease the baking tray with a little margarine. Sift the flour, bicarbonate of soda, ground ginger and ground cinnamon into a mixing bowl.

You will need:
Extra equipment:
a baking tray
cookie cutters
an icing syringe
a rolling pin

Ingredients:
350 g (12 oz) plain flour
1 teaspoon bicarbonate of soda
1 tablespoon ground ginger
½ teaspoon ground cinnamon
100 g (4 oz) butter
175 g soft brown sugar
1 egg

For the icing:
1 egg white
100 g (4 oz) icing sugar
food colouring

Preheat the oven to 180°C /
350°F / gas mark 4

Makes
15-20

2. Rub in the butter with your fingertips until it looks like breadcrumbs. Next, add the sugar.

3. In a separate saucepan or bowl, mix together the egg and golden syrup and then add to the dry ingredients. Mix together until it forms a dough.

4. Put the dough onto a floured surface and gently roll it out (not too thinly) with a rolling pin. Cut out shapes, putting them onto a baking tray as you go. Collect the dough trimmings into a ball and roll them out to make more biscuits. Bake in the oven for 10–15 minutes. Cool on a wire rack.

5. To make the icing, beat the egg white in a small bowl, and then sift the icing sugar on top. Beat the ingredients together until you have a smooth, stiff paste, and add a few drops of food colouring if you like. Spoon the icing into a syringe and decorate your gingerbread men!

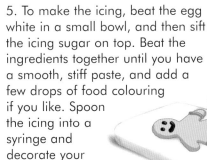

# Valentine Muffins

*Share these muffins with the people that you love!*

# Valentine Muffins

1. Use a paper towel to grease the baking tray with a little soft butter.

2. Put the butter, sugar, egg and flour into a large mixing bowl. Stir them all together with a wooden spoon until they are well mixed.

3. Sift the baking powder and cocoa powder into the bowl. Add the milk. Mix together.

**You will need:**
Extra equipment:
a muffin baking tray

**Ingredients:**
50 g (2 oz) butter
75 g (3 oz) brown sugar
1 egg
100 g (4 oz) plain flour
90 ml (3 fl. oz) milk
2 teaspoons baking powder
1 tablespoon cocoa powder
**For the topping:**
fresh whipped cream

Turn to the next page to find out how to make different Valentine Muffins.

Preheat the oven to 200°C / 400°F / gas mark 6

**Makes 12**

Top Tip!
Why not decorate each muffin with a little sugar heart?

4. Use a teaspoon to divide the mixture equally into the muffin tray. Bake the muffins for 12 minutes.

5. Leave the muffins in the tray until they are cool, and then decorate them with fresh whipped cream.

# Valentine Muffins

## Variation

1. Put paper cases in the muffin baking tray. Sift the flour into a bowl.

2. Put the margarine in the bowl. Use the tips of your fingers to rub the margarine and flour together until the mixture becomes crumbly.

3. Add the sugar and stir in the egg. Finally, add enough milk to make the mixture creamy.

4. Put spoonfuls of the mixture into the paper cases. Bake the muffins for 10–15 minutes, then leave them to cool on a wire rack.

5. Decorate them with a generous swirl of fresh whipped cream. Cover with coconut and a little sugar heart on top.

You will need:

Ingredients:
225 g (8 oz) self-raising flour
75 g (3 oz) margarine
75 g (3 oz) caster sugar
1 egg
75-100 ml (2-4 fl. oz) milk

For the topping:
fresh whipped cream
desiccated coconut
sugar hearts

# Fruit and Nut Slice

These spicy bars will give you enough energy to play for hours!

# Fruit and Nut Slice

1. Lightly grease the tin with a little butter and line it with a piece of greaseproof paper.

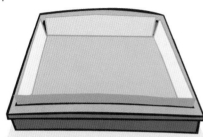

**You will need:**

Extra equipment:
a square tin 78 cm (7 in.)
greaseproof paper
an icing syringe

Ingredients:
100 g (4 oz) butter
75 g (3 oz) caster sugar
2 eggs
2 tablespoons black treacle
100 g (4 oz) plain flour
1 ½ teaspoons baking powder
1 teaspoon ground cinnamon
1 teaspoon mixed spice
225 g (8 oz) raisins
50 g (2 oz) chopped walnuts

Preheat the oven to 180°C /
350°F / gas mark 4

Makes
12

2. Put the butter and sugar into a large bowl and beat them together until they are light and creamy.

3. Beat the eggs together with a fork in a small bowl. Add them to the butter mixture, a little at a time, and mix them in well. Now mix in the treacle.

To decorate:
2 tablespoons icing sugar
2 teaspoons water

Top Tip!
Dip the spoon in hot water before measuring out the treacle – the treacle will slip off the spoon!

# Fruit and Nut Slice

4. Sift the flour, baking powder, cinnamon and spices into the bowl.

5. Stir in the raisins and walnuts.

6. Spoon the mixture into the tin and smooth the top with the back of the spoon. Bake for 15–20 minutes.

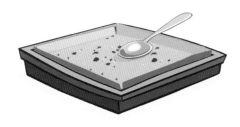

7. Remove the tin from the oven. When it is cool enough to touch, cut twelve bars from the mixture and transfer them to a wire rack.

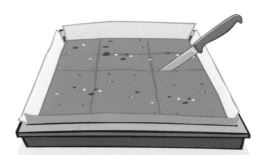

8. You can ice the bars when they are completely cool. Sift the icing sugar into a bowl and add the water, mixing well with a wooden spoon to make a thick paste. Spoon the icing into the icing syringe and decorate the bars with zigzag patterns.

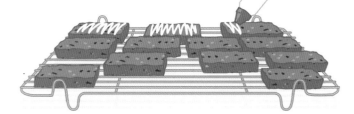

# Oat Cookies

*Mmm ... munch your way through these gorgeous oat cookies!*

# Oat Cookies

1. Use a paper towel to grease the baking tray with a little soft margarine. Put the margarine and sugar into a bowl and mix them together with a wooden spoon.

2. Add the flour and the oats to the bowl. Mix everything together, using a spoon and then your hands, to make a soft dough.

**You will need:**

Extra equipment:
a cookie cutter

Ingredients:
100 g (4 oz) soft margarine
75 g (3 oz) demerara sugar
100 g (4 oz) plain wholemeal flour
100 g (4 oz) porridge oats

Preheat the oven to 180°C / 350°F / gas mark 4

**Makes 8-10**

3. Put the dough onto a floured surface and gently press it out.

4. Cut out circles of dough and put them onto the baking tray.

5. Bake the cookies in the oven for 12–15 minutes, until they are golden brown. Place the cookies onto a wire rack to cool.

# Bread and Butter Pudding

*Layer upon layer of yumminess awaits you with this dessert!*

# Bread and Butter Pudding

## To make the custard:

1. Whisk the eggs, sugar and vanilla essence together. Then, slowly add the milk, whisking all the time.

## To make the pudding:

1. Cut the crusts off the bread and lightly butter each slice. Next, lay in a buttered pie dish in a neat overlapping pattern, and sprinkle with sultanas.

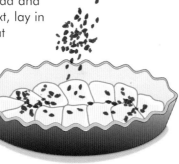

2. Partly cover the bread slices with some of the custard.

3. Leave to stand to allow the custard to soak in. Then, add the rest of the mixture and sprinkle with the caster sugar.

4. Wipe the edges of the dish and bake in a preheated oven for approximately 45 minutes–1 hour or until the custard is set and the bread is golden and crispy.

5. When the pudding has cooled slightly, brush with a little apricot jam. Serve warm!

## You will need:

**Extra equipment:**
an oven-proof pie dish
an electric whisk

**Ingredients:**
8 slices white bread
50 g (2 oz) butter
50 g (2 oz) sultanas
25 g (1 oz) caster sugar
25 g (1 oz) apricot jam
For the custard:
3 large egg yolks
2 tablespoons golden caster sugar
a few drops of vanilla essence
300 ml (10 fl. oz) milk

Preheat the oven to 180°C / 350°F / gas mark 4

Take Note!
Ask an adult to help you use the electric whisk.

Serves 4

# Coconut Cupcakes

*Exotic cupcakes with a cherry on top!*

# Coconut Cupcakes

1. Put the paper cases in the bun tin.

2. Combine the coconut, icing sugar, flour, baking powder and ground almonds in a large bowl.

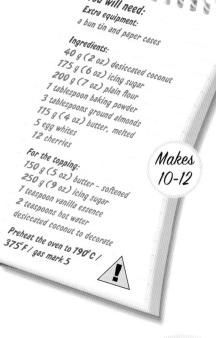

You will need:
Extra equipment:
a bun tin and paper cases

Ingredients:
40 g (2 oz) desiccated coconut
175 g (6 oz) icing sugar
200 g (7 oz) plain flour
1 tablespoon baking powder
3 tablespoons ground almonds
115 g (4 oz) butter, melted
5 egg whites
12 cherries

For the topping:
150 g (5 oz) butter - softened
250 g (9 oz) icing sugar
1 teaspoon vanilla essence
2 teaspoons hot water
desiccated coconut to decorate

Preheat the oven to 190°C /
375°F / gas mark 5

Makes
10-12

3. Stir in the melted butter. Stir in the egg whites, until well combined.

4. Use a teaspoon to transfer the mixture to the paper cases. Bake the cupcakes for 12–15 minutes. Leave them to cool on a wire rack.

5. For the topping, beat together the butter and icing sugar. Once well mixed, add the vanilla, food colouring and water. Beat until smooth and creamy.

*Top Tip!*
*Add a glacé cherry to the top of each cupcake to finish.*

6. Swirl the topping over your cupcakes, then sprinkle on desiccated coconut. Finish with a cherry on top.

# Rhubarb Crumble

*Tuck into this crumbly pudding classic!*

# Rhubarb Crumble

## To make the filling:

1. Grease an oven-proof pie dish with a little soft butter. Ask an adult to trim and wash the rhubarb and cut into 2½ cm (1 in.) pieces. Place in the bottom of the dish, sprinkle the sugar over the rhubarb, and stir.

**You will need:**
Extra equipment:
an oven-proof pie dish

**Ingredients:**
For the filling:
450 g (1 lb) pink rhubarb
180 g (6 oz) caster sugar

For the crumble:
100 g (4 oz) plain flour
50 g (2 oz) caster sugar
50 g (2 oz) butter

Preheat the oven to 190°C /
375°F / gas mark 5

Serves
6

## To make the crumble:

1. Sift the flour and 25 g (1 oz) of the sugar in a large bowl. Gently rub in the butter to form large breadcrumbs, taking care not to compact the mixture.

2. Scatter this mixture evenly over the rhubarb and sprinkle the remaining caster sugar over the top.

3. Bake in a preheated oven for approximately 30–40 minutes or until the crumble is golden and crisp.

# Apple Pie

*A traditional, comforting pie for you to prepare!*

# Apple Pie

## To make the pastry:

1. In a large bowl, combine the flour and caster sugar using your fingertips.

2. Gently rub in the butter until the mixture forms breadcrumbs.

3. Make a well in the centre and break in the egg. Mix carefully to produce a firm but crumbly pastry.

4. Cover with cling film and refrigerate for 20 minutes.

## To make the filling:

1. Ask an adult to melt the butter in a saucepan and then add the chopped apple.

You will need:
Extra equipment:
cling film
rolling pin
buttered pie dish

Ingredients:
For the pastry:
240 g (8½ oz) plain flour
50 g (2 oz) caster sugar
150 g (5 oz) butter
1 egg

For the filling:
25 g (1 oz) butter
450 g (1 lb) cooking apples, peeled and chopped
100 g (4 oz) caster sugar
½ teaspoon fresh grated nutmeg
1 pinch cinnamon

Preheat the oven to 190°C / 375°F / gas mark 5

Serves 6

Top Tip! Try using a different fruit filling.

# Apple Pie

2. Cook on a low heat under a tight-fitting lid, stir occasionally and cook until soft. Add the sugar, then the nutmeg and cinnamon to taste. Cover and allow to cool completely.

3. When the pastry is rested, divide into two pieces. Cover a buttered heatproof 20 cm (8 in.) pie dish with one half of the pastry rolled thinly.

4. Press gently into the base and sides and trim off any overlapping edges.

5. Prick the pastry base with a fork to prevent it rising. Add the cooked, cooled apple to the centre of the dish and smooth out to the edges.

6. Roll out the remaining pastry, dampen the edges of the pie with a little water. Lay the pastry over and trim the edges. Decorate the pastry by pinching the edges between the finger and thumb and make a steam hole in the centre. Bake in a preheated oven until the pastry is crisp and golden – approximately 25–30 minutes. Serve warm with cream, custard or ice cream.

# Dutch Apple Tart

*Mmm … this Dutch apple tart won't stick around for long!*

# Dutch Apple Tart

## To make the pastry:

1. Place the flours and sugar in a large bowl, add the butter and rub gently with your fingertips to form breadcrumbs.

2. Add the cold water and mix to a firm dough, cover and refrigerate to rest.

## To make the filling:

1. Ask an adult to slowly cook the apples in a saucepan with the butter, lemon zest and juice. Add the sugar and sultanas halfway through, stir and cover with a lid.

2. When cooked to a thick purée, allow the mixture to completely cool.

3. Cover a heatproof pie dish with half of the pastry using the method given for Apple Pie (see pages 54–55).

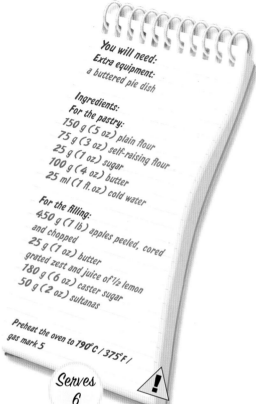

You will need:
Extra equipment:
a buttered pie dish

Ingredients:
For the pastry:
150 g (5 oz) plain flour
75 g (3 oz) self-raising flour
25 g (1 oz) sugar
100 g (4 oz) butter
25 ml (1 fl. oz) cold water

For the filling:
450 g (1 lb) apples peeled, cored and chopped
25 g (1 oz) butter
grated zest and juice of ½ lemon
180 g (6 oz) caster sugar
50 g (2 oz) sultanas

Preheat the oven to 190°C / 375°F / gas mark 5

Serves 6

4. Add the cold apple filling and cover with the remaining pastry. Crimp the edges to form a pretty effect, brush with cold water and sprinkle with caster sugar.

5. Make a steam hole in the centre of the tart and bake in a preheated oven until crisp and golden. Serve with cream, custard or ice cream!

# Honey and Pecan Tart

*The gooey honey and crunchy pecans make this pie a winner!*

# Honey and Pecan Tart

## To make the pastry:

1. Sift the flour and sugar into a large bowl, and carefully rub in the butter with your fingertips until it forms breadcrumbs.

2. Add the egg yolk and knead to form a firm dough. Cover with cling film and rest in the fridge for 20 minutes.

3. Thoroughly grease a flan tin with a loose base and line with the pastry. Leave the pastry edges overhanging until the pastry is well rested to avoid shrinkage, then ask an adult to trim the edges with a sharp knife.

4. Prick the base with a fork before lining with baking parchment. Fill with baking beans and cook in a preheated oven for 10–12 minutes.

5. Remove the paper and beans.

You will need:
Extra equipment:
a flan tin with a loose base
baking parchment
baking beans

Ingredients:
For the pastry:
100 g (4 oz) plain flour
15 g (½ oz) sugar
50 g (2 oz) butter
1 egg yolk

For the filling:
240 g (8½ oz) honey
150 g (5 oz) pecans
25 g (1 oz) breadcrumbs

Preheat the oven to
180°C / 350°F /
gas mark 4

Serves
4

# Honey and Pecan Tart

## To make the filling:

1. Ask an adult to melt the honey in a saucepan, add the pecans and simmer for 2 minutes.

2. Scatter the breadcrumbs in the base of the flan and pour the honey and pecan mixture over.

3. Smooth the surface and place in a preheated oven for 20–30 minutes, until the pastry is crisp.

4. Serve warm with cream or ice cream!

# Raspberry Towers

*These pretty layered biscuits will go down well at any party!*

# Raspberry Towers

## To make the shortbread:

**You will need:**
**Extra equipment:**
icing syringe, sieve,
rolling pin, baking parchment
electric whisk
a cookie cutter
**Ingredients:**
**For the shortbread:**
100 g (4 oz) butter
75 g (3 oz) caster sugar
160 g (5½ oz) soft flour
15 g (½ oz) ground rice
**For the filling:**
300 ml (½ pt) whipping cream
300 g (11 oz) fresh raspberries
small spray of fresh mint leaves
15 g (½ oz) icing sugar

Preheat the oven to **200°C /
400°F / gas mark 6**

Serves
4

1. Place the butter and sugar in a bowl and mix together well.

2. Sieve the flour and ground rice into the mixture and stir. Mix to a smooth dough, cover and chill in a refrigerator.

3. When cold and firm, divide into two halves and roll each using a dust of flour until it is 3 mm (¼ in.) thick.

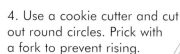

4. Use a cookie cutter and cut out round circles. Prick with a fork to prevent rising.

5. Line a baking tray with baking parchment and cook in a preheated oven until golden brown. Store in an airtight tin when completely cold.

# Raspberry Towers

## To make the towers:

1. Ask an adult to whip the cream until stiff.

*Take Note!*
*Ask an adult to help you use the electric whisk.*

2. Using an icing syringe and star nozzle, pipe a ball of cream in the centre of the shortbread.

3. Arrange the raspberries neatly around the cream and press another shortbread on top.

4. Repeat the process and pipe a neat ball of cream on the top and decorate with a single raspberry and a pair of mint leaves.

5. Place on a serving plate and dust with icing sugar.

# Scrummy Strudel

Prepare to impress your family and friends with this scrummy strudel!

# Scrummy Strudel

1. Line the work surface with a large clean cloth, lay three sheets of filo pastry side by side overlapping to form a large rectangle (see below).

2. Brush with melted butter and cover with the remaining three sheets. Then, brush these with melted butter too.

3. Lay a pile of chopped apple along the edge nearest to you but not quite reaching the sides, splash melted butter over the apple, scatter with the sugar, breadcrumbs and freshly grated nutmeg. Dust thickly with cinnamon.

You will need:

Extra equipment:
a large clean cloth

Ingredients:
6 sheets of filo pastry
50 g (2 oz) butter, melted
450 g (1 lb) cooking apples washed, peeled and chopped
50 g (2 oz) breadcrumbs
50 g (2 oz) caster sugar
freshly grated nutmeg
cinnamon
25 g (1 oz) apricot jam

Preheat the oven to 200°C / 400°F / gas mark 6

Serves
6

4. Starting at the edge with the apple mixture, gently lift the edge of the cloth and use it to help you roll the pastry lengthways. Lift this onto a baking tray and brush the top with melted butter.

5. Bake in a preheated oven until golden and crisp.

6. Remove from the oven and brush with warm apricot jam to make a glaze. Ask an adult to use a sharp knife to cut into slices while still warm.

# Mississippi Pecan Pie

*This pecan pie is so delicious, you'll want to make it again and again!*

# Mississippi Pecan Pie

## To make the pie case:

1. Make flan pastry by mixing the flours and sugar. Add the butter and gently rub with your fingertips until the mixture forms breadcrumbs. Mix in the egg to form a firm dough.

2. Cool and rest for an hour.

3. Use the dough to line a flan tin. Allow the edges to overhang until rested.

4. Line the pastry with baking parchment and fill with baking beans. Cook in a preheated oven for 10–12 minutes. Once cool, remove the baking beans.

You will need:
**Extra equipment:**
a flan tin, baking parchment, baking beans
**Ingredients:**
**For the pie pastry:**
75 g (3 oz) self-raising flour
25 g (1 oz) plain flour
25 g (1 oz) sugar
15 g (½ oz) butter
1 small egg
**For the filling:**
50 g (2 oz) butter
180 g (6 oz) golden syrup
50 g (2 oz) muscovado sugar
vanilla essence
3 eggs, lightly beaten
150 g (5 oz) pecans
Preheat the oven to 200°C / 400°F / gas mark 6

Serves 6

## To make the filling:

1. Ask an adult to heat the butter, golden syrup and muscovado sugar in a saucepan until they have melted.

2. Allow to cool, add the vanilla essence and eggs, mix in pecans and pour into the flan base.

3. Bake for 30–40 minutes, remove and allow to cool. Serve with cream!

# Ice Cream Strawberry Shortcake

*Eat these quick before the ice cream melts!*

# Ice Cream Strawberry Shortcake

## To make the shortcake:

1. Place the butter and sugar in a bowl and mix together well.

You will need:
Extra equipment:
sieve
baking parchment

Ingredients:
To make the shortcake:
100 g (4 oz) butter
75 g (3 oz) caster sugar
160 g (5 oz) plain flour
15 g (½ oz) rice flour
To make the filling:
approximately 4 balls of
vanilla ice cream
450 g (1 lb) strawberries

Preheat the oven to 200°C /
400°F / gas mark 6

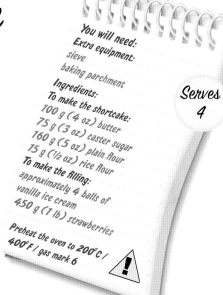

**Serves 4**

2. Sieve in the flour and rice flour and add to the butter mix. Mix together to make a smooth paste, cover and chill.

3. Divide the mixture into eight even-sized balls and place on a baking tray lined with baking parchment. Bake in a preheated oven until crisp and golden. As soon as they are baked, sprinkle with a little more caster sugar whilst still hot.

## To make the filling:

1. When the shortcake is cold, sandwich with small balls of vanilla ice cream.

2. Alternate the layers with halves of small strawberries, and then decorate the top with more ice cream and strawberries.

# Baked Blueberry Cheesecake

*This fab, fruity cheesecake is great for any occasion!*

# Baked Blueberry Cheesecake

You will need:
Extra equipment:
a sponge tin
a blender
baking parchment

Ingredients:
150 g (5 oz) crushed digestive biscuits
50 g (2 oz) butter (melted)
180 g (6 oz) cottage cheese
150 g (5 oz) natural yogurt
1 teaspoon plain flour
15 g (½ oz) caster sugar
1 egg plus 1 egg white
juice and grated zest of half a lemon
200 g (7 oz) blueberries
mint leaves

Preheat the oven to 180°C / 350°F / gas mark 4  ⚠

**Serves 4**

1. Grease and line a tin with a little butter and baking parchment. Mix the digestive biscuits and melted butter together and spoon into the tin. Chill until firm.

2. Place the cottage cheese in a blender and ask an adult to whizz until smooth.

3. Add the cottage cheese to a bowl and mix in the yogurt, flour, sugar, egg and egg white. Stir gently, then mix in the lemon zest and juice, and fold in the blueberries, saving a few for decoration.

4. Pour the mixture onto the biscuit base and bake in a preheated oven for 30–35 minutes or until just set. Turn off the oven and leave for another 30 minutes.

5. Ask an adult to run a knife around the cheesecake and carefully turn out onto a serving plate. Decorate with the remaining blueberries and mint leaves.

Top Tip! Instead of blueberries, you could use raspberries, blackcurrants or strawberries.

# Strawberry Ginger Snaps

*Strawberries give these crunchy ginger snaps that little extra something!*

# Strawberry Ginger Snaps

1. Ask an adult to melt the butter, sugar and syrup in a small pan. Stir in the flour and ginger, add the grated rind of the half lemon and 1 tablespoon of the juice.

2. Place 12 tablespoons of the mixture well spaced on baking parchment. Bake them in a preheated oven for 8–10 minutes until golden. Allow to cool slightly, and then slide off the paper onto a wire rack.

3. Ask an adult to whip the cream with the icing sugar until it forms soft peaks.

*Take Note! Ask an adult to help you use the electric whisk.*

4. Spoon fresh cream into the middle of one ginger snap, surround with fresh strawberries and sandwich with a second ginger snap. Repeat with a third, and decorate the top with cream and a single strawberry.

5. Repeat the process to produce three more strawberry ginger snaps.

# Lemon Cheesecake with Strawberries and Blueberries

*This mouth-watering cheesecake is simple to make!*

# Lemon Cheesecake with Strawberries and Blueberries

You will need:

Extra equipment:
23 cm (9 in.) loose-bottomed tin
baking parchment
plastic food bag
rolling pin
electric whisk
spatula

Ingredients:
250 g (9 oz) digestive biscuits
100 g (4 oz) butter, melted
1 vanilla pod
600 g (1 lb, 3 oz) soft cheese
60 g (2 oz) caster sugar
100 g (4 oz) icing sugar
grated zest and juice of 1 lemon
240 g (8½ oz) strawberries
115 g (4 oz) blueberries

**Serves 12**

**Take Note!** Ask an adult to help you use the electric whisk.

1. Butter and line a loose-bottomed tin with baking parchment. Then, put the biscuits in a food bag and crush using a rolling pin.

2. Transfer the crumbs to a bowl, then pour over the melted butter. Mix thoroughly until the crumbs are completely coated.

3. Tip them into the tin and press firmly down into the base to create an even layer. Chill in the fridge for 1 hour to set.

4. Ask an adult to prepare the vanilla pod by scraping out the seeds.

5. Next, place the soft cheese, icing sugar, lemon juice and zest and vanilla seeds in a bowl, then ask an adult to beat using an electric mixer until smooth. Tip in the cream and continue until combined.

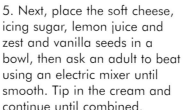

6. Cut the strawberries in half and stand around the base. Next, spoon the mixture onto the base. Smooth with a spatula and leave to set in the fridge.

7. Arrange the rest of the strawberries around the top edge and fill the centre with blueberries.

8. Place the base on top of a plate, then pull the sides of the tin down, removing the paper and base.

# Jammy Almond Muffins

*Make these fruity treats for your whole family to enjoy!*

# Jammy Almond Muffins

1. Use a paper towel to grease the muffin tray with a little soft butter.

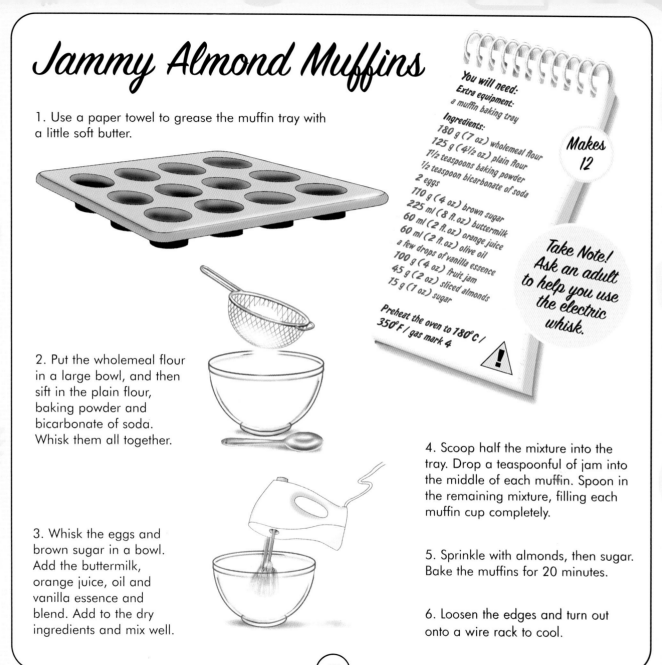

You will need:
Extra equipment:
a muffin baking tray

Ingredients:
180 g (7 oz) wholemeal flour
125 g (4½ oz) plain flour
1½ teaspoons baking powder
½ teaspoon bicarbonate of soda
2 eggs
110 g (4 oz) brown sugar
225 ml (8 fl. oz) buttermilk
60 ml (2 fl. oz) orange juice
60 ml (2 fl. oz) olive oil
a few drops of vanilla essence
100 g (4 oz) fruit jam
45 g (2 oz) sliced almonds
15 g (1 oz) sugar

Preheat the oven to 180°C / 350°F / gas mark 4

Makes 12

Take Note!
Ask an adult to help you use the electric whisk.

2. Put the wholemeal flour in a large bowl, and then sift in the plain flour, baking powder and bicarbonate of soda. Whisk them all together.

3. Whisk the eggs and brown sugar in a bowl. Add the buttermilk, orange juice, oil and vanilla essence and blend. Add to the dry ingredients and mix well.

4. Scoop half the mixture into the tray. Drop a teaspoonful of jam into the middle of each muffin. Spoon in the remaining mixture, filling each muffin cup completely.

5. Sprinkle with almonds, then sugar. Bake the muffins for 20 minutes.

6. Loosen the edges and turn out onto a wire rack to cool.

# Scrummy Savoury Recipes

*Scrummy savoury recipes for you to bake and enjoy!*

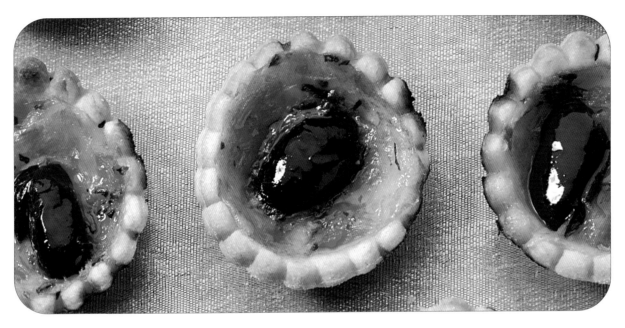

# Classic Sausage Rolls

*A classic sausage roll recipe for the whole family to enjoy!*

# Classic Sausage Rolls

**You will need:**
Extra equipment:
a rolling pin
a pastry brush

Ingredients:
1 tablespoon butter
1 red onion, peeled and finely sliced
6 pork sausages
a handful of breadcrumbs
2 tablespoons plain flour
250 g (10 oz) ready-made puff pastry
1 egg
a little milk

Preheat the oven to 180°C / 350°F / gas mark 4

Makes 10

1. Melt the butter in a saucepan and add the onions. Cook gently for about 20 minutes until soft and golden brown. Then, spread out on a plate to cool.

2. Ask an adult to slit the skins of the sausages and pop the meat out. Put the meat in a mixing bowl with the onion and the breadcrumbs, and then scrunch well, with clean hands, to mix together.

3. On a floured work surface, roll the pastry out into a rectangle so it is about 1 cm (½ in.) thick. Then, cut it lengthways into two long, even rectangles. Roll the mixture, made in step 2, into sausage shapes with your hands, and lay along the centre of each rectangle.

4. Mix the egg and milk and brush over the pastry. Then, fold one side of the pastry over the filling. Press down with your fingers or the edge of a spoon to seal.

5. Cut the long rolls into the size you want and space them out on a baking tray. Brush with the rest of the egg and bake for 25 minutes or until puffed and golden.

# Perfect Pizzas

*An authentic Italian mini pizza recipe!*

# Perfect Pizzas

1. Empty the pizza base mix into a bowl, add the water, and mix, according to the packet instructions.

2. Using a rolling pin, roll the pizza mix dough so it is about 2 cm (1 in.) thick. Use the cookie cutters to cut out shapes.

**You will need:**
*Extra equipment:*
cookie cutters

*Ingredients:*
290 g (10 oz) pizza base mix
100 ml (3 ½ fl. oz) warm water
tomato purée
mozzarella cheese
any topping you like
basil or oregano (optional)

*Preheat the oven to 200°C / 400°F / gas mark 6*

Makes
20

3. Next, spread the tomato purée onto the base, then add the mozzarella cheese and the herbs.

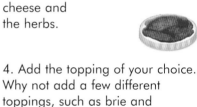

4. Add the topping of your choice. Why not add a few different toppings, such as brie and cranberry or perhaps a sweet topping like pineapple!

5. Ask an adult to place the mini pizzas into a pre-heated oven for 10–15 minutes or until they are piping hot and the bases are golden brown!

# Pastry Parcels

*Cheese and cranberry make these pastry parcels a taste sensation!*

# Pastry Parcels

1. Ask an adult to cut each piece of filo into four quarters and also to cut the brie into four.

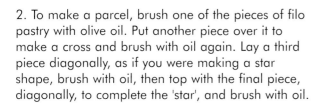

You will need:
Extra equipment:
pastry brush

Ingredients:
4 sheets of pre-made filo pastry
200 g (8 oz) brie
4 tablespoons of olive oil
4 heaped teaspoons of cranberry sauce

Preheat the oven to 200°C / 400°F / gas mark 6

2. To make a parcel, brush one of the pieces of filo pastry with olive oil. Put another piece over it to make a cross and brush with oil again. Lay a third piece diagonally, as if you were making a star shape, brush with oil, then top with the final piece, diagonally, to complete the 'star', and brush with oil.

Makes
4

3. Place one of the pieces of brie in the centre of the pastry and put a heaped teaspoon of cranberry sauce on top of it. Fold up the sides of the filo and scrunch them at the top so they hold together. Brush all over with olive oil. Make three more parcels in the same way.

4. Place all of the parcels on a lightly oiled baking sheet and bake in the oven for 15–20 minutes, or until crisp and lightly browned.

# Cheesy Straws

*Quick and easy to make, these delicious cheesy straws are best eaten while they are still warm from the oven!*

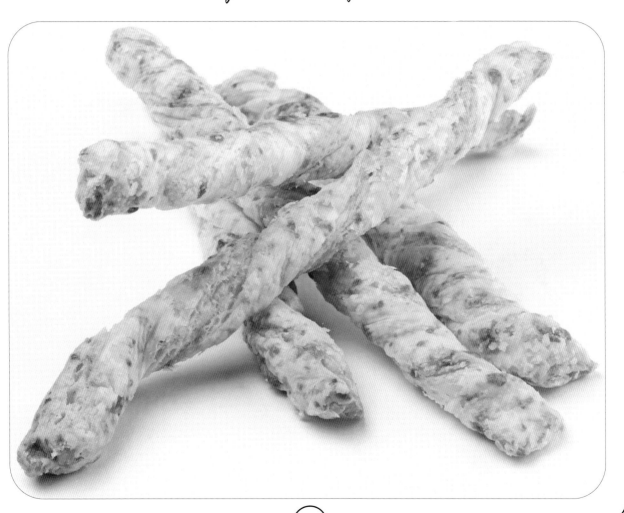

# Cheesy Straws

1. Grease a baking tray with a little butter and cover it with a piece of baking parchment.

You will need:

Extra equipment:
baking parchment
sieve
rolling pin

Ingredients:
100 g (4 oz) butter
150 g (5 oz) mature cheddar cheese, or a mixture of cheddar and parmesan
100 g (4 oz) plain flour
1 free-range egg yolk

Preheat the oven to 200°C / 400°F / gas mark 6

Makes 24

2. Grate the cheese into a bowl and then sift in the flour with a sieve.

3. Cut the butter into small cubes and rub them into the mixture with your fingers. When the mixture is crumbly and the butter has almost disappeared, stir in the egg yolk.

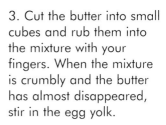

6. Ask an adult to place the baking tray into a preheated oven and bake for about 7 minutes or until the cheesy straws are a pale golden brown.

4. Next, roll the pastry into a ball. Then, dust the work surface with plenty of flour and roll out the pastry into a rough square that is 5 mm thick.

5. Cut the square into strips and transfer them onto the baking tray. Ensure that you leave a small space between each one.

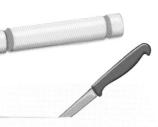

7. Transfer the cheesy straws to a wire rack and allow to cool.

# Tomato and Cheese Tartlets

*This finger food will go down a treat at any sleepover!*

# Tomato and Cheese Tartlets

1. Sift the flour and salt into a bowl and add the butter. Rub the butter with your fingers until the mixture resembles fine breadcrumbs.

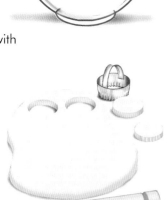

2. Add enough water to make a smooth dough, kneading lightly. Cover with cling film and put into the fridge for 30 minutes. Roll out on a floured surface to 0.5 cm (¼ in.) thick. Use a cookie cutter to cut out circles of pastry and line the tartlet trays. Leave in the fridge for 30 minutes.

**You will need:**

Extra equipment:
a cookie cutter, tartlet tray, cling film, rolling pin, container

Ingredients:
For the tartlet cases:
225 g (8 oz) plain flour
a pinch of salt
50 g (2 oz) butter
1-2 tablespoons cold water
For the tomato filling:
1 tablespoon olive oil
1 small onion, very finely chopped
400 g (14 oz) tin of chopped tomatoes
pinch dried oregano
½ teaspoon sugar
To finish the tartlets:
700 g (4 oz) mozzarella cheese, thinly sliced
10 black olives, pitted and cut in half (optional)
a little olive oil

Preheat the oven to 200°C / 400°F / gas mark 6  ⚠

**Makes 20**

3. Prick the base of each tartlet with a fork and bake in a preheated oven for 5 minutes. Cool and store in a container until needed.

4. To make the filling, ask an adult to put the oil into a small saucepan over a medium heat. Add the onion and cook gently for 4–5 minutes until soft. Add the tomatoes, oregano, and sugar. Cook for another 5–7 minutes, stirring occasionally until thick. Set aside to cool.

5. Put the pastry cases back into the tartlet trays and put a teaspoon of the mixture in each one. Put a piece of mozzarella cheese on top of each tartlet, followed by half an olive, if using. Brush with oil and bake in the oven for 5–7 minutes, until the cheese has melted. Serve warm!

# Cheese Scones

*These super scones are perfect as an after school treat!*

# Cheese Scones

You will need:
Extra equipment:
rolling pin
a cookie cutter

Ingredients:
225 g (8 oz) self raising flour
pinch of salt
50 g (2 oz) butter
25 g (1 oz) mature cheddar
cheese, grated
150 ml (5 fl. oz) milk

Preheat the oven to 200°C /
400°F / gas mark 6

Makes
8-12

1. Lightly grease a baking tray.

2. Mix together the flour and salt and rub in the butter.

3. Stir in the cheese, followed by the milk to create a soft dough.

4. Knead the dough on a floured work surface. Then, roll out the dough until it is 2 cm (½ in.) thick. Then, use a cookie cutter to cut out the scones and place them onto the baking tray.

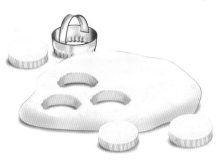

5. Brush the top of each scone with a little milk. Ask an adult to place them into a preheated oven and bake for 12–15 minutes or until they have risen and are a nice golden colour.

6. Transfer the scones onto a wire rack and allow to cool.

# Corn Cakes

*A simple recipe that's easy to whip up for breakfast!*

# Corn Cakes

1. Use a paper towel to grease the muffin tray with a little soft butter.

2. Mix the butter and sugar in a medium mixing bowl. Add the cornflour and vinegar. Stir them all together until they are well mixed.

3. Add the water. Then, stir in the flour and polenta.

4. Mix everything together well until just moistened.

5. Use a teaspoon to divide the mixture equally into the muffin tray. Bake the muffins for 20 minutes.

6. Leave the muffins in the tray until they are cool, and then turn out and enjoy.

**You will need:**

Extra equipment:
a muffin baking tray

Ingredients:
50 g (2 oz) butter
50 g (2 oz) sugar
2 tablespoons cornflour
2 tablespoons vinegar
250 ml (8 fl. oz) water
190 g (7 oz) plain flour
125 g (5 oz) polenta

Preheat the oven to 200°C / 400°F / gas mark 6

Makes 10-12

Top Tip!
To soften the butter, take it out of the fridge at least 30 minutes before cooking.

# Your Recipes

# Your Recipes

# Your Recipes

# Your Recipes